Simple 1-2-3™

COLOR & FRAME

≫3 BOOKS IN 1≪

W0009957

new seasons®
a division of Publications International, Ltd.

ISBN: 978-1-64558-761-3

Manufactured in China.

8 7 6 5 4 3 2 1

Let's get social!

@Publications_International

@PublicationsInternational

www.pilbooks.com

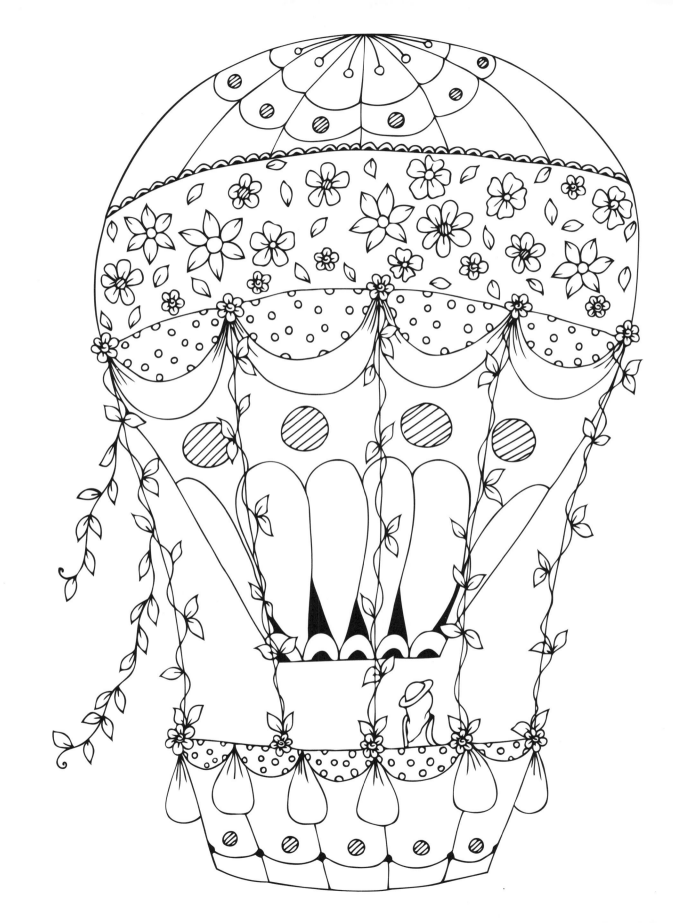

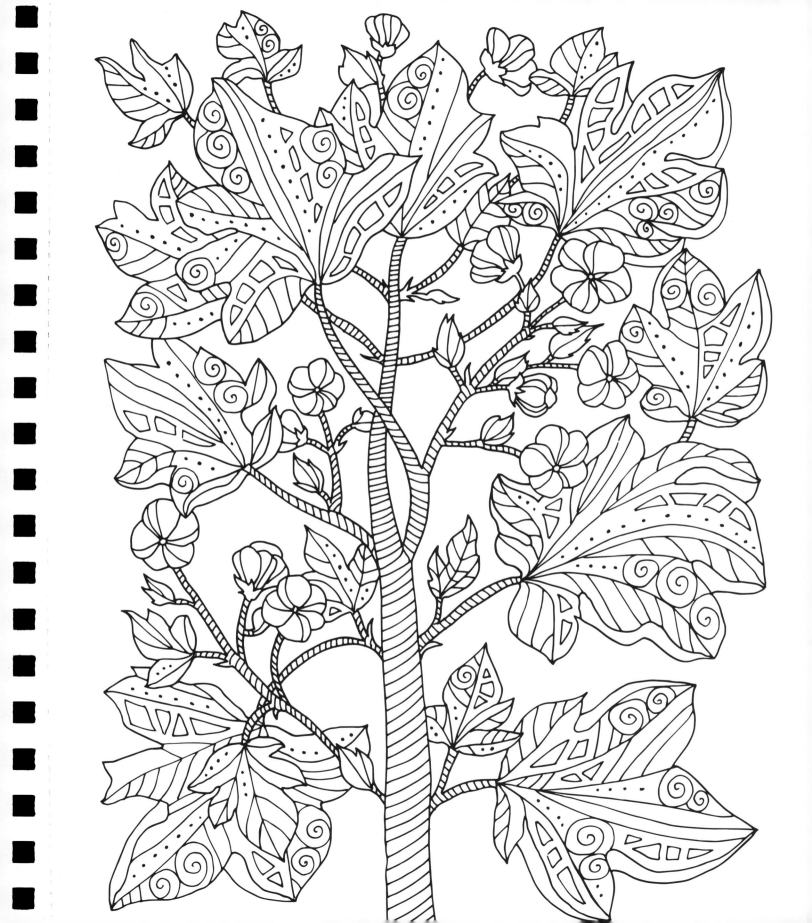

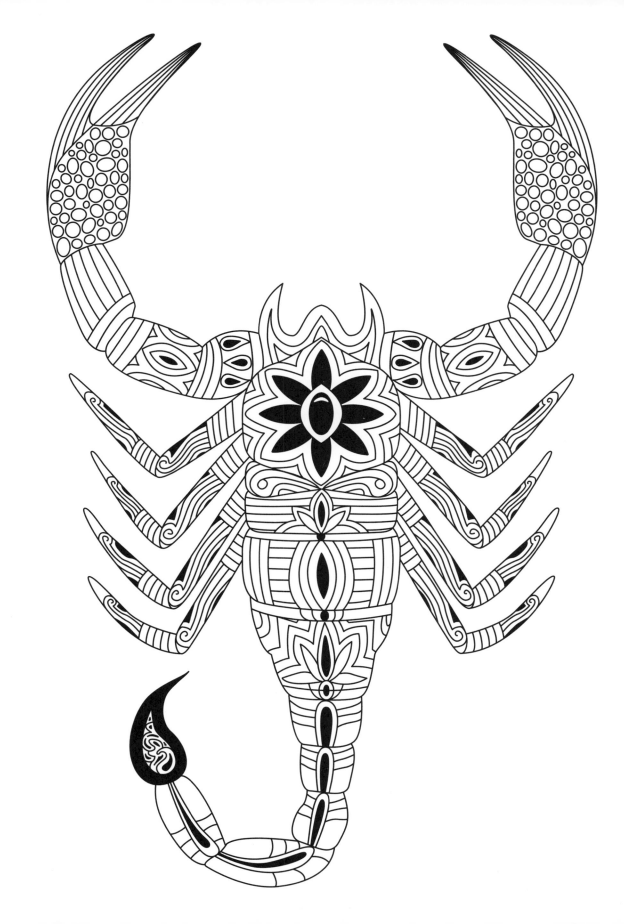

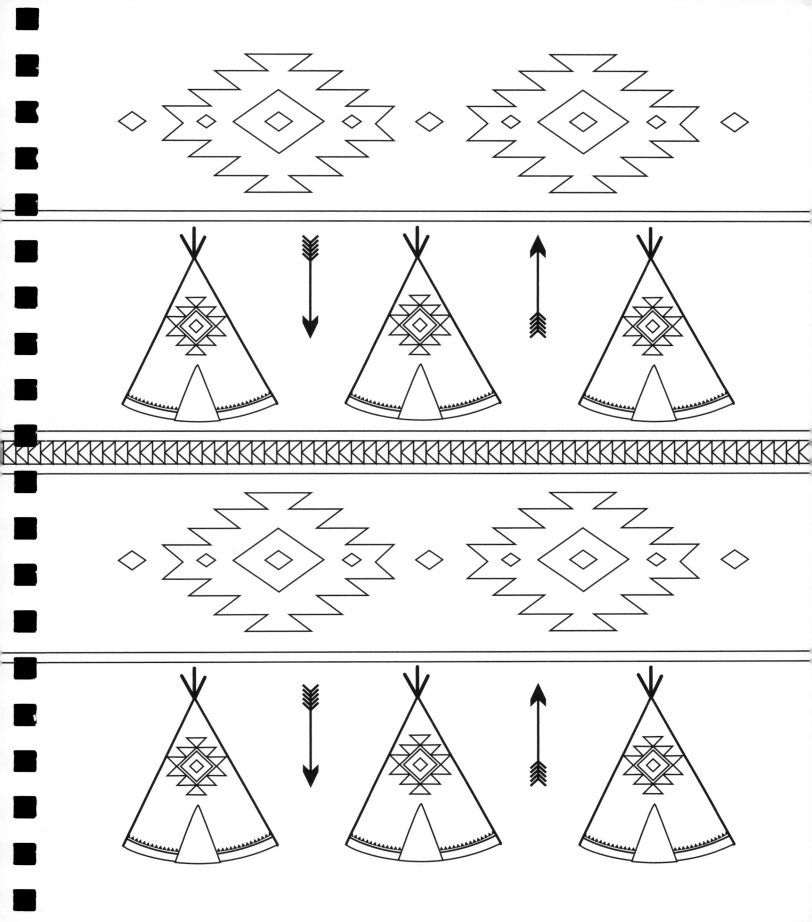

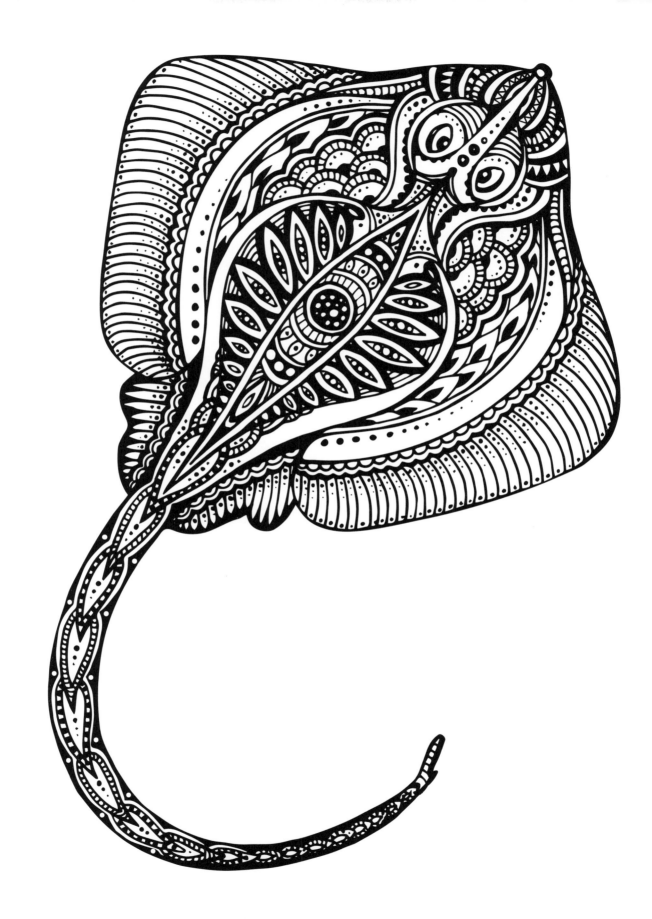

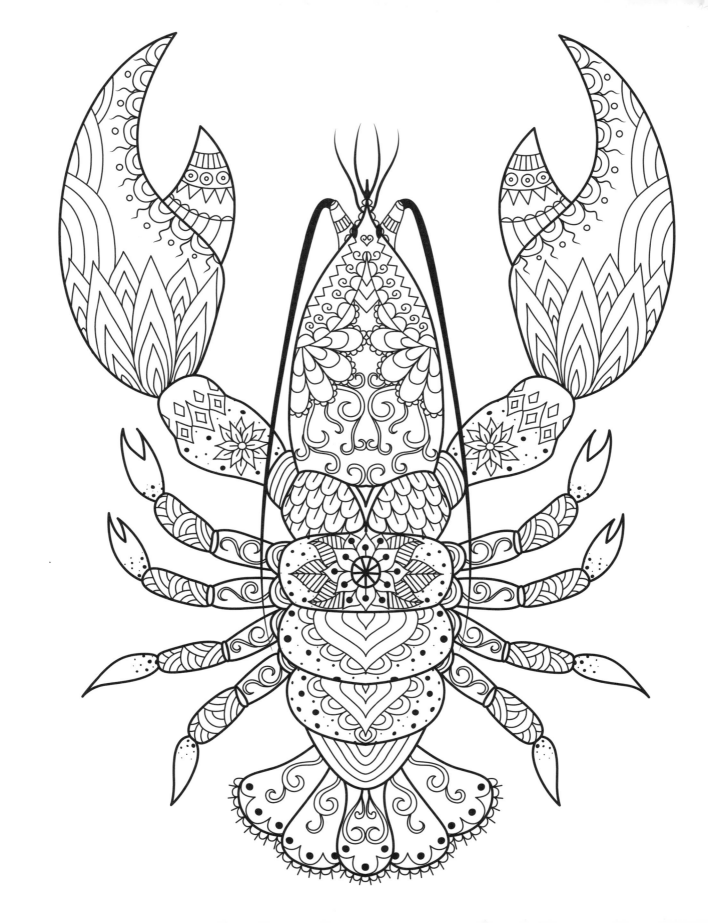